GOOD HOUSEKEEPING
NEEDLEPOINT

GOOD HOUSEKEEPING
NEEDLEPOINT

EBURY PRESS

Chief Contributor
Dorothea Hall

Art Editor
Sue Rawkins

Editor
Miren Lopategui

Assistant
Lesley Prescott

Managing Editor
Amy Carroll

Managing Art Editor
Debbie Mackinnon

Good Housekeeping Needlepoint
was conceived, edited and designed by
Dorling Kindersley Limited, 9 Henrietta Street, London WC2E 8PS

First published in Great Britain in 1981 by
Ebury Press
Division of the National Magazine Company Limited
Colquhoun House
27-37 Broadwick Street
London W1V 1FR

Second impression 1982
Third impression 1983
Fourth impression 1984
Fifth impression 1986

ISBN 0 85223 202 0

Printed in Singapore

Contents

❖

❖

Introduction

Needlepoint – embroidery on canvas – is currently
one of the most popular forms of embroidery, a relaxing
pastime enjoyed equally by both men and women.
The attraction that canvas embroidery has seems partly due to
the simple order involved in counting the threads as the
stitches are worked, and the fact that a modest canvas mesh
can be quickly transformed into a very handsome fabric.
One of the oldest types of embroidery known,
canvas work has, throughout history, reflected contemporary
trends in design. Early examples from the Middle Ages,
called *Opus pulvinarium*, or cushion work, show that free
embroidery stitches and couching were all mixed with counted
stitches within the same coarse-linen embroidery.
However, English embroidery of the late seventeenth,
eighteenth, and nineteenth centuries was mostly worked in one
stitch only – small stitches, such as tent stitch (petit point),
gros point and cross stitch – describing perfectly the realism
of the currently popular designs. Many stitches were
invented at this time in imitation of the very expensive
tapestries that were being woven, and took their
names from tapestry-weaving towns such as Gobelin
and Aubusson in France. The introduction of stiff canvas
further divided the counted stitch from free-style embroidery
worked on soft linen, such as we work today.
The popularity of canvas embroidery over the last century
was stimulated by a number of craft revivals, notably by William
Morris at the turn of the century in England – a far-reaching
influence still dominant in the areas of wallpaper
and textile design today. It was the great craft revival
of the 1950s, however, which established embroidered
canvas not only as a practical craft, seen in clothes and
carpets, but as an art form, where large abstract
and three-dimensional designs displayed experimental
techniques and unconventional stitches.
The stitches and stitch patterns in the book range from the
traditional "tapestry" stitches through star, leaf and loop
stitches to beautiful Bargello patterns and border designs.
Accompanied by clear stitch diagrams and suggestions for their
interpretation and use, the illustrations have been
carefully chosen to reflect the
colour and design trends of today.

EQUIPMENT & TECHNIQUES

THREADS

In addition to the many specially produced tapestry yarns, most weaving, knitting, crochet and embroidery threads may be used for needlepoint. The type of thread used will depend on the ultimate use of the finished article. The thickness of the thread should be equal to the size of the canvas mesh you plan to use, and the finished embroidery should cover the canvas threads completely. Wool is a very hard-wearing fibre, with the unusual facility for "wearing clean", and is therefore particularly suitable for needlepoint. Tapestry yarns are available in a wide colour range and different thicknesses.

Crewel wool is a very fine, firmly-twisted 2-ply yarn which can be used singly on the finest canvas, or in multiple strands as required for heavier canvases.

Tapestry wool is a softly-twisted yarn, equivalent to a good 4-ply knitting weight.

Persian yarn is made up of three 2-ply strands loosely twisted together. These can easily be separated into single or varying numbers of strands.

Thrums are off-cuts from carpet weaving manufacturers made from thick 2-ply yarn, roughly equivalent to double-knitting weight; they are mothproof, hard-wearing and usually bought, fairly cheaply, as mixed thrums.

Rug wool is chunky, loosely-twisted 4- or 6-ply yarn, specially produced for rug making; though hard-wearing, it has a limited colour range.

Soft embroidery thread is loosely-twisted cotton with a matt finish; it is thinner than tapestry yarn.

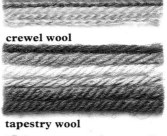

crewel wool

tapestry wool

persian yarn

thrums

rug wool

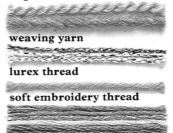

weaving yarn

lurex thread

soft embroidery thread

stranded cotton

7

NEEDLES

Tapestry needles are especially made for embroidering on canvas. They have an elongated eye, tapered shank and a round point, and can be bought in a range of sizes from 24 to 13. There is no precise rule for which size needle should be used with which size canvas but, generally speaking, you should choose a needle slightly thicker than your working thread. Your needle should be small enough to pass easily through the holes in the canvas without forcing the threads apart, but, equally, large enough for the yarn to move freely through the eye, and to carry the yarn through the canvas without fraying.

CANVAS

All needlepoint embroidery is worked on a canvas foundation fabric. The best canvas is made from polished linen or cotton threads and has an even weave of open mesh squares. It is woven either as single thread canvas or double thread canvas, in either écru or white. Choose an écru canvas for working dark colours and white for working light colours.

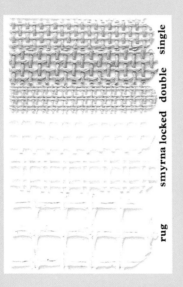

single
double
smyrna locked
rug

Single thread canvas (mono canvas) *is produced in a range from 32 to 10 threads per 2.5cm, the number of threads determining the number of stitches that will be worked over 2.5cm of canvas. Therefore, choose the canvas with the greater number of threads to 2.5cm for working fine detail into your needlepoint, and vice versa.*

Double thread canvas (Penelope canvas), Smyrna and rug canvas *– in order of coarseness – are made in a range from 18 to 3 holes per 2.5cm respectively, the number of holes determining the number of stitches that will be worked over 2.5cm of canvas. Choose double thread canvas (Penelope) for crossed stitches and for tramming designs. This canvas can be converted to single simply by pressing the threads apart with the needle; use it for combining design details in smaller stitches with a background of larger stitches. Smyrna or rug canvas are best for chunky needlepoint. Smyrna canvas may be used as double canvas, or single canvas by stitching between each double thread. Included in the rug canvas range are a number of "locked" double canvasses. These are useful for thrums; work as single canvas.*

FRAMES

Although a frame is not an essential piece of equipment, there are advantages in using one. A frame will keep the canvas evenly stretched, so that both hands are free and can therefore work more quickly. It also facilitates the use of the correct up and down movements to stitch; the canvas retains its shape and your stitches will be uniform in size throughout. Many frames are designed especially for needlepoint and are available in varying sizes (measured across the roller tape), but any square or oblong frame may be used. A beginner might even use an old picture frame, fastening the canvas in place with drawing pins.

Travel frame, *as its name suggests, is a light frame designed for carrying. It is made in two widths – 30.05cm and 61cm – by one standard depth of 30.05cm. The canvas is attached in the same way as described for the slate frame, rolling on and re-lacing it as required.*

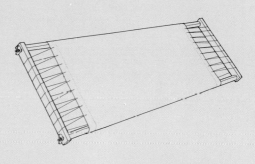

Straight-sided frame (slate frame) *This frame has two rollers, each with a piece of tape firmly nailed along its length, and two flat laths which slot into the rollers and are held with pegs or screws. The canvas is firmly stitched to the tape and any excess length wound tightly around one roller (before the pegs are inserted) and, finally, laced to the sides with fine string. To work the extra canvas, unlace, wind the canvas on and re-lace. This frame needs to be supported at each side at a comfortable height, with a floor stand, or against the side of a table.*

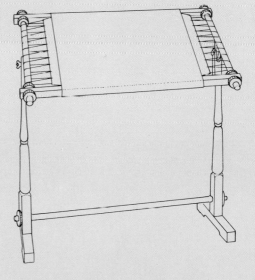

TRANSFERRING DESIGNS

You may easily work a simple design directly onto canvas by counting the threads and placing the stitches in a regular way. To embroider a more complicated design it is better to work from a coloured pattern which can be transferred to your canvas. Transfer the outline, and either use your original coloured pattern as a colour guide, or fill in the colours with waterproof acrylic paint. An easy way to do this is by using a sheet of glass placed between two kitchen chairs with a strong lamp underneath.

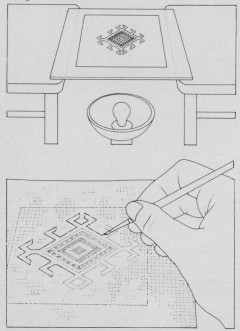

1 Attach your coloured pattern to the glass with masking tape. Place your canvas centrally on top, making sure that the canvas threads line up with any horizontal or vertical lines in your design, and tape to the glass.

2 Use a fine brush and waterproof ink, or waterproof marker, to outline the design. You can correct any mistakes with white acrylic paint. Note that it is often possible to transfer your design onto canvas by tracing through without the lamp underneath.

MAKING A CHART

Instead of painting your design onto the canvas, you may prefer to chart it on graph paper and transfer it to canvas by counting the squares as you embroider, each square of the graph paper representing one square of canvas mesh. Colour your design using felt-tipped pens. Textured stitches can be charted with additional symbols.

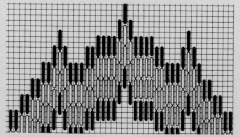

A simple Florentine pattern charted on graph paper with 16 squares to 2.5cm for working on 16 single thread canvas. The pattern repeats every 24 squares across by 3 rows of colour.

LARGE DESIGNS

Since one width of canvas may not be wide enough for some very big designs, such as those for carpets, it will be necessary to work them in sections and then sew them together later. This is no more difficult to do than any other needlepoint but some careful planning is needed. Remember to buy, or reserve, sufficient yarn of the same dye-lot, since seaming would show up badly matched colours.

First draw out the whole design on paper (or chart it on graph paper, see p.10), and then divide it into equal sections and label each one.

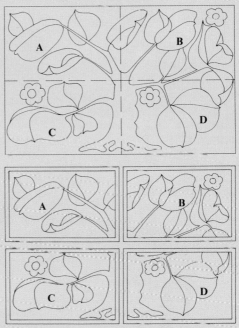

Cut equivalent pieces of canvas allowing an extra 7.5cm all round each piece and label them. Hem raw edges or cover with masking tape. Transfer design to corresponding piece of canvas, or read from chart, and embroider.

JOINING

As each section is completed, it should be blocked and set ready for stitching together. Use button thread for sewing fine canvas and carpet thread for heavier canvas. Begin by joining sections A and C together, then B and D, and finally stitch the two halves together making a vertical centre seam.

Fold back the unworked canvas on the top edge of section C and place it face upwards on top of the unworked canvas at the bottom of section A, matching pattern and placing close to stitching. Pin and tack in position. Slip stitch into each canvas mesh, pulling thread firmly. Remove pins and tacks and repeat for other seams. Work matching needlepoint stitches over seams, through single canvas only.

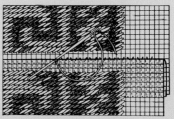

TRAMMING

A trammed design is first worked in coloured horizontal stitches over which the needlepoint is then worked in corresponding colours. Use tramming for transferring a design or for adding extra padding to stitches. This makes a very hard-wearing fabric, suitable for chair-seat upholstery. On Penelope canvas tramming stitches are worked horizontally in between the double threads in the colour shown on the pattern or painted on the canvas.

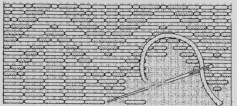

Work a simple geometric pattern in single tramming stitches to show a three-coloured design.

Split tramming on Penelope

If the area to be trammed is too big for one stitch to cover, then make several stitches; insert the needle through a double thread intersection and bring out to left through the stitch just worked. Do the same when a colour change occurs.

Tramming single canvas

On single canvas tramming stitches are worked between the horizontal threads and over as many vertical threads as required in a single colour. Should you need to make several stitches, insert the needle and bring it out 1 thread back and through the stitch just made. For trammed Upright Gobelin stitch see page 15.

DIAGONAL TENT STITCH

Use for describing very fine detail and also for working large areas of background where a well-padded stitch is required. You will see that the back of the canvas is also completely covered and is therefore a particularly useful stitch for hard wear. This method of working tent stitch is recommended wherever possible, since it does reduce the risk of the finished canvas being pulled out of shape.

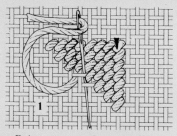

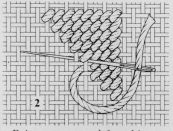

1 *Bring yarn out, insert needle diagonally upwards over 1 intersection. Pass needle vertically downwards behind 2 horizontal threads and bring out ready for next stitch.*

2 *Bring yarn out to left and insert needle upwards over 1 intersection, pass needle behind two vertical threads and bring out ready for the next stitch.*

BLOCKING

Even if you have managed to keep your needlepoint straight and clean while working it will still need blocking to give it that smooth and even look of new fabric. Blocking larger or smaller cannot change the actual size of your needlepoint, but it will correct any distortion that may have occurred while working, and restore the canvas to its original condition. Before you begin, draw the correct outline of the embroidered area onto a piece of blotting paper (to absorb moisture when sponged). As you stretch the canvas, check with the outline to get the exact shape.

SETTING

After blocking, the needlepoint is given its permanent shape by setting. To do this, lightly sponge the back of the embroidery with water and leave it to dry at room temperature away from strong sunlight (the water releases the gum coating on the canvas threads and re-sets as the needlepoint dries). Where the canvas has been badly distorted, it may require repeated settings, and perhaps a final coating of a mild solution of starch.

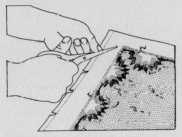

1 *First cover a clean, soft board with plastic, put the paper marked with the correct outline on it and the needlepoint on top, placed face downwards. Snip the selvedge so that the canvas will stretch evenly.*

2 *Lightly hammer in a single tack into the canvas margin at the centre top. Pull the canvas gently, making sure that the threads are at right angles to each other, and tack the centre bottom. Repeat this process on the two sides.*

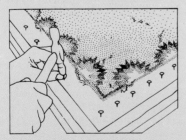

3 *Easing the needlepoint into the correct shape and working from the centre towards the corner on all edges, lightly insert more tacks at 2.5cm intervals.*

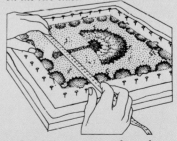

4 *Carefully measure and match canvas to correct shape, adjusting tacks where necessary. Dampen areas requiring a lot of stretching. Finally, hammer tacks securely.*

USEFUL TIPS

Calculating yarn: The exact amount of yarn needed to cover a given area of canvas varies with the coarseness of the canvas, and with the particular stitch you plan to use. Work a 2.5 cm square on your chosen canvas, estimate the total area to be stitched and then calculate how much you will need. Buy all your yarn at the same time, especially large background amounts, from the same dye-lot.

Calculating canvas: Always choose the most appropriate canvas type and the width best suited to the article you intend to work. In calculating the total amount, always add an extra 5 to 7cm all round, to facilitate stretching in a frame and to ease blocking.

Preparing your canvas: Turn in the edges of the canvas and machine-stitch, or cover the raw edges with masking tape. This prevents the canvas from fraying and the thread from catching.

THREADING YOUR NEEDLE:

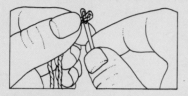

Fold the end of the yarn over the eye of the needle, and withdraw it, still holding the yarn tightly. Ease the eye of the needle over the fold and pull through.

Thread length: Your working thread should not be longer than 45 to 50cm. This avoids unnecessary wear as it passes through the canvas threads, and minimizes twisting and untwisting.

The correct twist: As you work, your yarn may twist in the needle and not cover the canvas well. Prevent this happening by passing the needle point downwards under the yarn, and giving it a half turn to left, before making the next stitch. Otherwise, lift the canvas and let the needle hang loose, when it will quickly unwind.

Starting and finishing off: Begin by making a long horizontal stitch under the row you are about to work and make the first 3 or 4 stitches over it. Finish off by running the needle under the last 3 or 4 stitches on the wrong side before cutting the yarn. Avoid knots.

Stitching: Work all stitches in two movements, with one hand on top inserting the needle downwards while the other hand returns it from underneath.

Tension: Work evenly throughout, keeping yarn relaxed and correctly twisted and allowing it to fill the canvas threads completely.

Planning your stitches: Whenever possible, try to plan your rows of stitches so that the needle comes up through an empty hole and goes back through a filled one. This gives a smoother finish and prevents odd strands of yarn being brought up from the wrong side.

Half stitches: To shape motifs or fill background areas, it may be necessary to work half stitches to fit (see tinted areas of diagrams).

Hand-held canvas: If you have to work your needlepoint in your hand then working will be made easier if you roll the canvas. Start from the bottom and roll it to a point close to your working area and fasten the sides, knotting a length of thread through the mesh.

STRAIGHT STITCHES

These are the simplest of all needlepoint stitches to work, adding subtle and decorative textures to your embroidery. You will see how easily they build up into patterns, and how fast they cover the canvas without distorting it. Remember that stitches that are too long will snag and are less hard-wearing than shorter ones. Rib, wave and twill textures contrast with smooth-sided triangles and pebbly effects. See also pp. 75, 92 and 94.

Upright gobelin stitch

Materials Crewel, tapestry or persian yarn, thrums or rug wool for a firm, close-ridged fabric; embroidery thread for a soft, ribbed texture.
Uses Satchel, rug or floor-cushion inset panel, or all-over repeat for box-sided cushion or chair seat; belt, bag or braces motif.

First work a trammed stitch from left to right and bring needle out 1 thread below. Insert needle 2 threads above and return to front 2 threads down and 1 thread to left. Continue to end of row. Pass needle of last stitch diagonally behind 3 horizontal threads and bring out 1 thread to left, and repeat. This stitch may be worked without a trammed thread (see p. 12).

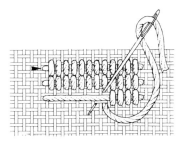

Gobelin filling stitch

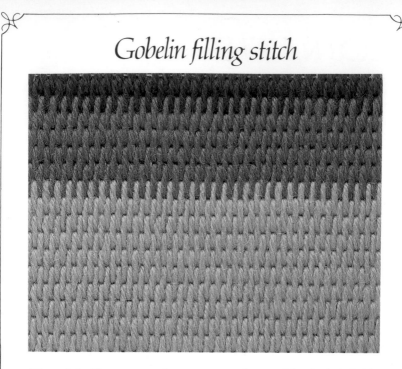

Materials Tapestry wool or rug yarn for a softly shaded finish; random-dyed embroidery thread for a gently mottled effect.

Uses All-over background pattern for wall panel, stool top, cushion set or chunky bedside rug; "keepsake" greetings card or herb pillow.

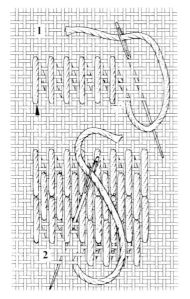

1 *Begin at top left and work a row of straight stitches upwards over 6 threads leaving 2 threads between each one.*

2 *Work second row from right to left fitting stitches evenly into previous row. Continue working each successive row in the same way.*

Parisian stitch

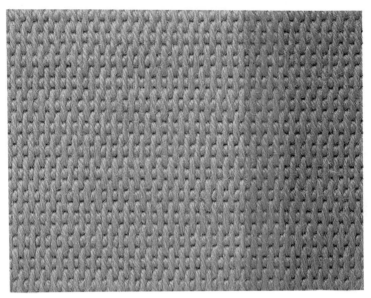

Materials Medium-weight tapestry yarn for a light, pebbly look; embroidery cotton or silk for a fine-textured finish.

Uses All-over stitch for games board (backgammon, checkers or chess), bag or bolster border; repeat pattern for sunglasses case.

Begin at either top left or right and work straight stitches alternately over 6 threads and 2 threads to end of row. Work each successive row so that the length of the stitches alternates evenly with previous row.

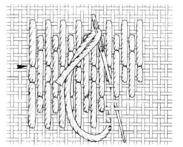

Algerian filling stitch

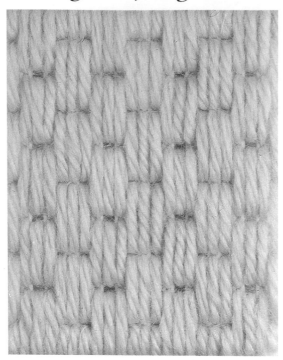

Materials Chunky rug yarn for a quick-to-work, deep-textured effect; tapestry wool for neat infilling.

Uses Inset panel for Aran-type rug, floor-cushion set or shoulder bag; cushion inset panel, border, or geometric motif.

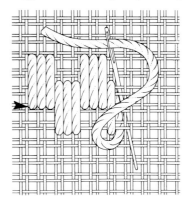

Start at top left and work 3 straight stitches upwards over 6 threads. Bring needle out 3 threads below and 1 thread to right. Work 3 stitches upwards over 6 threads, bring needle out 3 threads above and 1 thread to right. Continue in this way working second and subsequent rows in an opposite direction, fitting the stitches evenly into previous row.

Twill pattern

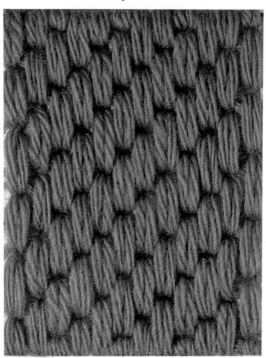

Materials Heavy-weight rug yarn or mixed knitting yarn oddments (work several strands together) for a rich embossed effect.
Uses Rug inset panel or border, or all-over pattern for work-bag or padded coffee-pot cosy.

Begin at bottom left and work each row diagonally to top right. Make 2 straight stitches upwards over 3 threads. Bring needle out 2 threads down and 1 thread to right.
Continue in this way to end of row and repeat.

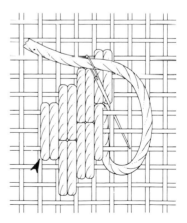

Renaissance stitch

Materials Soft embroidery thread, crewel wool, tapestry yarn or rug thrums for a neat, firm finish.

Uses All-over stitch for games-table top (mounted under glass), lamp-base cover, chair seat, piano bench cover or cushion set.

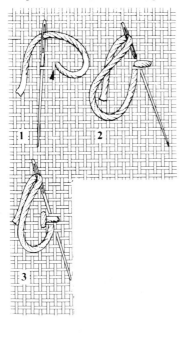

1 Work in a downward direction. Bring yarn out at top left, insert needle 2 threads to left and bring through 1 thread down.

2 Insert needle 2 threads up and pull through 2 threads down and 1 thread to right.

3 Insert needle 2 threads up and bring through 3 threads down and 1 thread to right, ready for working the next group of stitches.

Long stitch

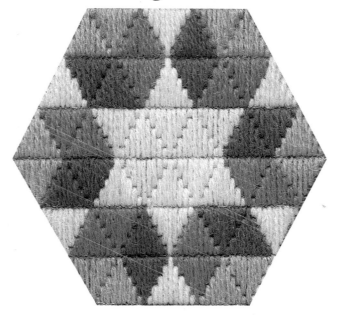

Materials Medium-weight tapestry wool, persian yarn or soft embroidery cotton for a decorative geometric effect.

Uses Cushion set or stool inset panel, picture frame border or all-over pattern for workbox lid or Christmas stocking.

Begin at top left and work a row of straight stitches in sequence over 10, 8, 6, 4, 2, miss 1 space, 2, 4, 6 and 8 horizontal threads. Work a second row of stitches in reverse sequence to fit evenly into the previous row. Repeat these two rows throughout.

Long stitch variation

Materials Stranded cotton, silk or soft embroidery thread for a fine brocade effect; tapestry wool for wear.

Uses Background stitch for landscape picture, purse or prayer book cover; all-over repeat for cigarette-lighter cover, or chair seat.

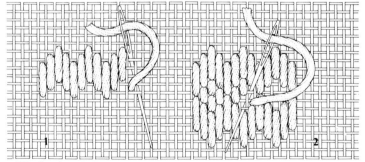

1 *Work a foundation row of straight stitches in wave pattern. Begin at top left and work first 3 stitches stepped upwards over 4 threads and back 3, then work the next 2 stitches back under 5 threads and upwards over 4. Continue to work these 2 stitches in wave pattern to end of row. Work a second row in reverse sequence.*

2 *Work 4 straight stitches upwards over 2 threads, to fit in the spaces left.*

Graduated straight stitch

Materials Embroidery thread, tapestry yarn, weaving wool or rug thrums for a colourful, pictorial effect.

Uses All-over stitch for landscape or portrait picture, wall decoration firescreen or tennis racket cover.

Bring yarn out at top left, insert needle the required distance away to the right and bring through 1 thread below the starting point. Continue making horizontal stitches in this way, adjusting the length of the stitch to fit the design. Turn canvas through 90° to work vertical graduated straight stitches.

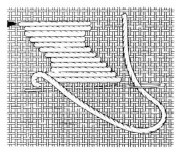

Encroaching straight stitch

Materials Soft embroidery cotton, tapestry yarn or crewel wool for a free-style graphic finish.

Uses All-over stitch for landscape, still-life or flower picture, wall-hanging, cushion inset panel or "keepsake" anniversary card.

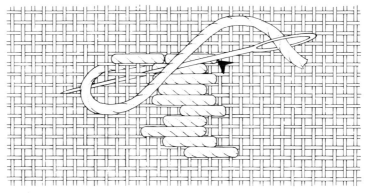

Begin at top right and, working downwards, make a series of horizontal straight stitches each varying in length. Insert the needle over a random number of vertical threads to the right, bringing it through 1 thread below, near the starting point. Complete the first vertical row. Work a similar row upwards, fitting each stitch neatly to the left of the stitches in the previous row. Continue in this way until your required area is complete.

DIAGONAL STITCHES

All these stitches cover the canvas mesh well. The smallest diagonal stitches adapt perfectly to backgrounds, or to describing the finest detail, while longer sloping stitch textures show movement, direction and shading.

Tent stitch

Materials Crewel or tapestry wool, rug thrums or chunky yarn for both detail and hard wear; silk or cotton threads for fine graphic description.

Uses All-over stitch for portrait picture, coat of arms, chair seat, fireside rug or stool top; bookmark, lapel badge or button set.

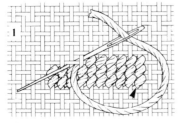

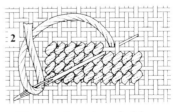

1 *With yarn at right, insert needle diagonally upwards over 1 intersection and bring it out 1 thread down and 2 threads to left. Continue to end of row.*

2 *The second row is worked from left to right passing the needle diagonally upwards. All stitches should slope in the same direction.*

Half cross stitch

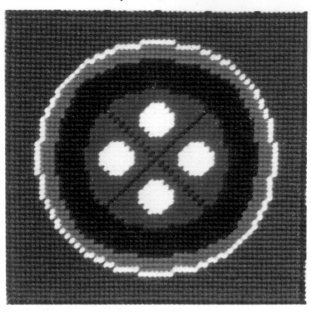

Materials Soft embroidery thread, tapestry wool or persian yarn for fine detail and yarn economy.

Uses All-over stitch for games board (mounted under glass), cushion set, piano stool cover, envelope purse or shoulder bag.

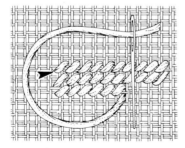

Bring yarn out at top left, insert needle diagonally to right over 1 intersection of double mesh canvas. Pass needle behind in downward direction and pull through 1 double thread down. Continue to end of row. Turn canvas upside-down to work second row and repeat.

Aubusson stitch

Materials Medium-weight embroidery cotton or tapestry wool for graphic detail and a firm, ribbed fabric.

Uses All-over stitch for chair seat inset panel, crest motif on slippers or spectacle case, initialled belt, badge or baby's soft building block.

1 *Begin at top left, and bring yarn through in between 1 horizontal double thread. Insert needle diagonally to right over 1 vertical double thread and bring out in wide space below starting point.*
2 *Make a second diagonal stitch, inserting needle in between horizontal double thread to right and bringing through in between horizontal double thread down to left, and repeat as shown.*

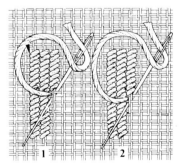

Gobelin stitch

Materials Tapestry wool or persian yarn for durability; silk, cotton or soft embroidery thread for bright fashion accessories.

Uses Dining chair set, floor-cushion, kneeler or rug panel; dress yoke or blouson inset panel, purse or pocket motif.

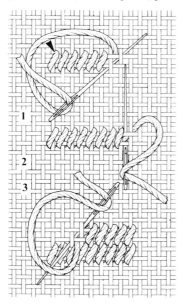

1 *Working from left to right, bring yarn out at bottom left and make a diagonal stitch over 2 threads down and 1 thread to left. Pass needle diagonally behind and bring out 2 threads up and 1 thread to right. Repeat to end of row.*

2 *For second row, insert needle vertically upwards under 2 threads.*

3 *Work from right to left passing needle diagonally downwards from above. Continue to the end of the row and repeat.*

Encroaching gobelin stitch

Materials Random-dyed or plain embroidery thread, crewel or tapestry wool for a softly shaded effect.
Uses All-over background stitch for miniature landscape or portrait picture, girl's dress yoke, purse or special birthday card.

Working from right to left, make a row of diagonal stitches downwards over 5 threads and 1 thread to left. For second row, work from left to right making diagonal stitches in the same way, overlapping the previous row by 1 horizontal thread. Continue in this way, working each row alternately from right to left, and from left to right.

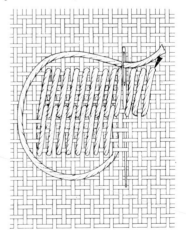

Reversed sloping gobelin stitch

Materials Crewel or tapestry wool, persian yarn or rug thrums for a firm, woven-textured fabric.
Uses Satchel or cushion inset panel, or all-over pattern for chair seat, square pouffe, foot stool or rug border.

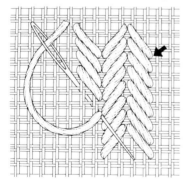

Work vertically downwards, starting at arrow. Make a row of diagonal stitches taking the needle upwards over 2 double thread intersections to left. Pass needle diagonally behind and bring out 1 double thread down and 2 double threads to right. Work the stitches of the second, and every alternate row, at right angles to the first, starting at bottom left.

Knitting stitch

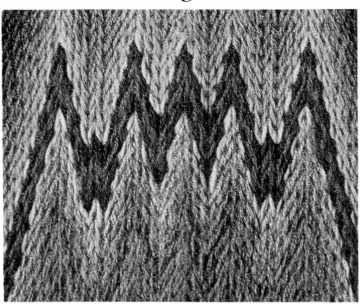

Materials Medium-weight silk or cotton thread, crewel or tapestry wool for ribbed, "stocking stitch" texture.

Uses Coat or dress yoke, waistcoat, purse or cushion inset panel, or all-over "Florentine" pattern for bolster, bag or book cover.

1 *Work vertically, beginning at bottom right. Insert needle 4 threads up. Bring out 2 threads down and 1 thread to left. Continue to the end of the row.*
2 *Finish off last stitch of first row by inserting needle 4 threads up and bringing out 2 threads to left.*
3 *Work second row downwards in reverse, inserting needle 4 threads down. Bring out 2 threads up and 1 thread to left.*

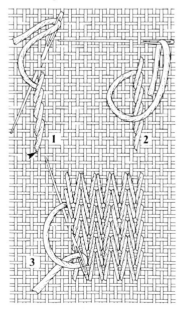

Portuguese diamond stitch

Materials Soft embroidery thread or tapestry wool for a bright over-check effect.

Uses Dress yoke or inset panel, or repeat pattern for cushion set, brick book-end cover, slippers or egg-cosy.

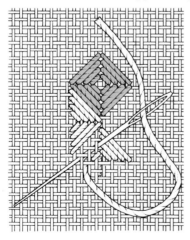

Work a series of diagonal stitches to form 4 triangles obliquely arranged into 1 large diamond. Begin at centre top and work downwards in sequence over 4, 3, 2 and 1 thread to right. Pass needle of last stitch under 2 threads to left, and work second triangle in reverse sequence upwards over 1, 2, 3, and 4 threads to left. To complete diamond, turn work upside-down and repeat.

Diagonal mosaic stitch

Materials Soft embroidery cotton, tapestry wool or persian yarn for a light, speckly texture.

Uses Cushion or rug inset panel; all-over pattern for book cover, or desk set (blotter frame, pencil holder and diary cover).

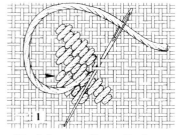

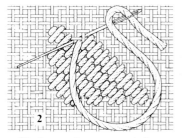

1 *Work first row diagonally from top left to bottom right. Bring yarn out to left and work diagonal stitches to right, over 1 and 2 threads alternately.*

2 *Work second row upwards from bottom right to top left, neatly placing the longest stitch diagonally above the shortest stitch of the previous row.*

Diagonal stitch

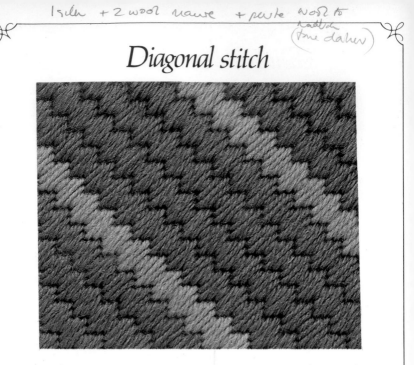

Materials Crewel wool, tapestry or persian yarn for a stripy, textured fabric.

Uses Inset panel for leather-trimmed satchel or purse, bolster or rug; all-over pattern for waistcoat, wallet or coffee-pot cosy.

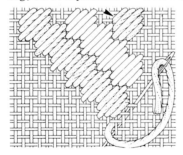

Work from top left to bottom right. Make a series of diagonal stitches in sequence over 2, 3, 4, and 3 intersections of thread. Work the second, and subsequent rows below, placing the longest stitches diagonally in line with the shortest stitches of the previous row.

Cashmere stitch

Materials Crewel wool, stranded yarn, knitting oddments or tapestry wool for a firm, nubbly-textured fabric.
Uses Single motif for nursery picture or child's badge, or all-over stitch pattern for boy or girl cushion and matching rug border.

1 *Work from bottom right to top left. Make a series of diagonal stitches in sequence over 1, 2, and 2 intersections of thread, working each group of stitches 1 thread to left as shown.*
2 *Similarly, work the second row in the opposite direction and in the same sequence, moving each group of stitches 1 thread to left.*

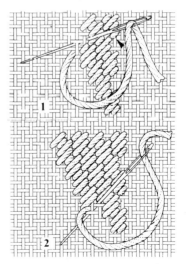

Byzantine stitch

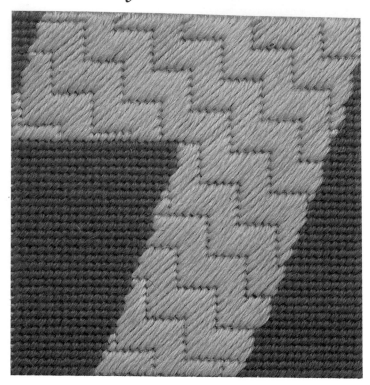

Materials Tapestry or persian yarn for hard wear plus a classical look; silk or cotton embroidery thread for a smooth finish.

Uses Repeat number or alphabet motif for child's cushion and rug set, or baby's soft building block; initialled teenage pocket or purse.

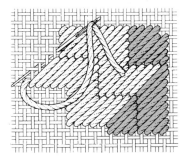

Begin at bottom right and work 5 diagonal stitches to the left over 4 threads up and 4 threads across, followed by 5 diagonal stitches worked vertically over 4 threads up and 4 threads across. Continue in this way, repeating the stepping sequence in each successive row.

Milanese stitch

Materials Crewel wool, tapestry, persian or rug yarn for a formal brocade effect; silk or stranded cotton for mounting under glass.
Uses All-over pattern for cushion set, chair upholstery, inset rug panel, or large motif infilling; wall panel or games board.

Make a series of diagonal back stitches to form 4 alternating triangles worked over 4 rows. Bring yarn out at top right and work back stitches diagonally downwards in the following sequence; first row, over 1 and 4 intersections alternately; second row, over 2 and 3; third row, over 3 and 2, and fourth row, over 4 and 1 intersection alternately. Continue to repeat these 4 rows in sequence.

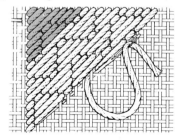

Reversed stem stitch

Materials Tapestry wool, carpet thrums, persian yarn or rug wool for a hard-wearing, closely-woven finish.

Uses Pouffe, stool or rug inset panel, or all-over pattern for bolster, doorstep, workbox top, golf club cover or tote bag.

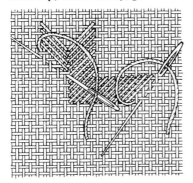

Work a series of oblique diagonal stitches arranged to form a cross. Bring yarn out at centre top and insert needle up to right over 4 intersections of thread and bring out 5 threads down and 4 to left. Working vertically downwards, make 8 more diagonal stitches, then work 8 diagonal stitches to right over 4 intersections of thread. Work top left section of cross in reverse. Turn canvas upside-down to work second half of cross in reverse. Into each tip of the cross, work a triangle of straight stitches in sequence over 8, 6, 4, and 2 threads. Work subsequent crosses in diagonal rows, each one fitting neatly into the spaces made by the previous cross.

CROSSED STITCHES

*There are, in addition to the popular
cross stitch, many other attractive and very
distinctive variations. Most of them are extremely
hard-wearing and the regular appearance is obtained by
making sure that all the stitches cross in the same direction.
This group of stitches has the most versatile range of
textures, from the pebbly look of a single cross,
to knotted and plaited bands, and two-colour reverse.*

Cross stitch

Materials Silk, stranded cotton or crewel wool for describing fine detail; tapestry or rug wool for a firm, hard-wearing fabric.
Uses Motif for pretty "keepsake" picture, valentine or anniversary card; all-over stitch for chair set, floor-cushion or rug.

1 *Work horizontally from right to left. Bring yarn out to right, insert needle up to left over 1 double thread intersection and bring out 1 double thread down.*
2 *Insert needle diagonally upwards 1 double thread intersection to right and bring needle through again in the same place, ready to make the next stitch.*

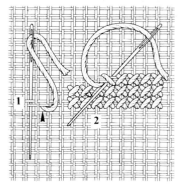

Diagonal cross stitch

Materials Stranded cotton or silk thread for infilling a simple motif; tapestry wool or chunky rug yarn for wear.

Uses Greetings card motif, or all-over pattern for child's stuffed toy, purse or egg-cosy; fireside rug inset panel or cushion set motif.

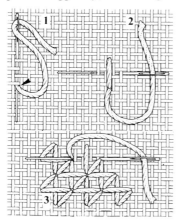

1 *Work diagonally from bottom right to top left. Bring yarn out at arrow, insert needle 4 threads up and pull through again at arrow.*

2 *Insert needle 2 threads up and 2 threads to right, bring out 4 threads to left.*

3 *Make a back stitch over 4 threads to right, bring needle out in the same place, ready to begin the next stitch. Work the next and subsequent rows above, fitting each cross neatly into the spaces made by the stitches in the previous row.*

Upright cross stitch

Materials Soft embroidery or stranded cotton for a child's practice piece; crewel wool or tapestry yarn for a close-textured finish.
Uses Motif for child's purse, satchel badge or pencil case; all-over pattern for ladybird-shaped cushion or nursery rug panel.

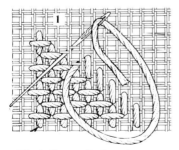

1 *Work diagonally from bottom right to top left. Bring yarn out and make a row of stepped vertical stitches. Insert needle over 2 horizontal double threads and bring out 1 double thread intersection down to left.*

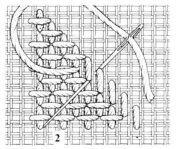

2 *On return journey, make a row of stepped horizontal stitches. With yarn at left, insert needle over 2 vertical double threads, crossing the previous stitch, and bring it out 1 double thread intersection down to left.*

Oblong cross stitch

Materials Persian yarn, carpet thrums or rug wool for a quick, decorative effect.

Uses Inset panel for wall-hanging, bathroom or bedside rug, or all-over pattern for padded tea- or coffee-pot cosy.

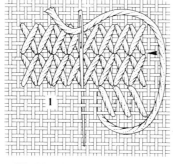

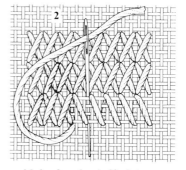

1 *Working horizontally from right to left, bring yarn out and insert needle 4 threads up and 2 threads to left. Bring out 4 threads down, forming a half oblong cross. Continue to end of row.*

2 *Make the other half of the cross on the return journey, working from left to right, over the same group of threads. Work subsequent rows below, fitting the crosses directly under those of previous row.*

Reversed cross stitch

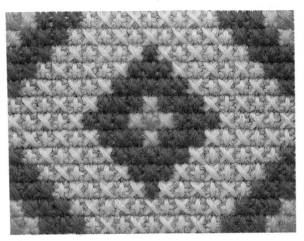

Materials Soft embroidery cotton, crewel wool or tapestry yarn for a pretty, embossed effect.

Uses Repeat motif for napkin ring, egg-cosy, belt, mirror frame or cushion border; all-over pattern for shoulder bag or bolster.

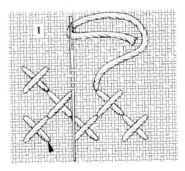

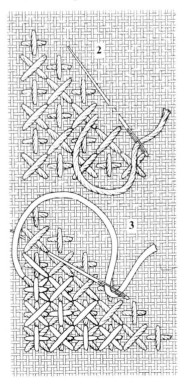

Work diagonal rows of cross stitch and upright cross stitch in alternate sequence, superimposed by cross stitches.

1 *Begin at bottom left and work diagonal cross stitch over 4 intersections of thread, leaving 4 threads between each row.*

2 *Work upright cross stitch over 4 threads between the rows already worked.*

3 *With the same, or contrast yarn, work crosses over the basic stitches in reverse sequence.*

Rice stitch

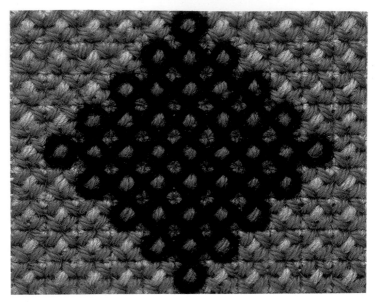

Materials Tapestry wool, persian yarn, thrums or chunky wool for a rich colourful effect.

Uses Inset panel or border for mixed-stitch chunky rug and matching cushion set, stool top, door-stop or shoulder bag.

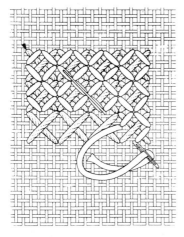

Working horizontally, begin at top left and cover your required area with rows of cross stitch worked over 4 intersections of thread. Then, with the same, or contrast thread, make the return journey working diagonal back stitches over each corner of the crosses. Work the back stitch over 2 intersections of thread.

Smyrna cross stitch

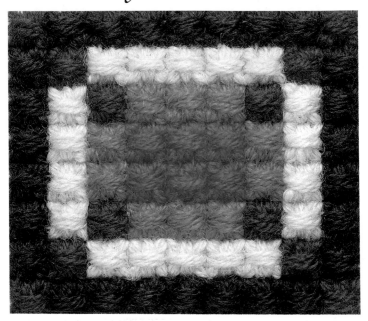

Materials Medium to heavy-weight yarn for a deep embossed texture; stranded or soft embroidery cotton for a pretty, pearly effect.
Uses Inset panel for bed head or "patchwork" cushion set, bolster or rug border; all-over stitch for party purse or curtain ties.

1 *Start at top left and work in horizontal rows. Bring yarn out and make a cross stitch as shown, over 4 intersections of thread. Bring needle out 4 threads down and 2 threads to right.*
2 *Insert needle 4 threads up and bring out 2 threads down and 2 threads to left.*
3 *Insert needle 4 threads to right and bring out 2 threads down, ready to work next stitch.*

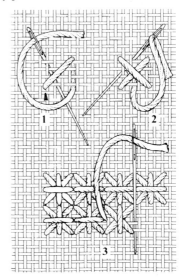

Alternating cross stitch

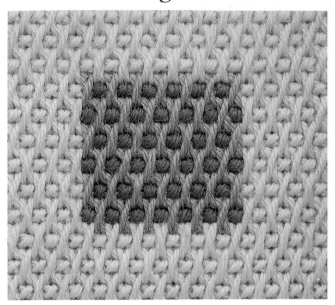

Materials Soft embroidery thread, crewel wool or tapestry yarn for a quick decorative finish.
Uses Dress yoke or inset panel, or all-over pattern for cushion set, child's pencil-case, egg-cosy or napkin ring.

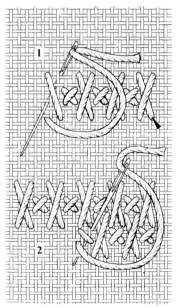

Work rows of oblong cross stitch and cross stitch alternately in 1 or 2 colours.
1 *Begin at top right and work horizontally. Bring yarn out and make an oblong cross stitch over 6 threads up and 2 threads to right; then bring needle out 4 threads down and 2 threads to left.*
2 *Make a cross stitch over 2 intersections; bring needle out 4 threads down and 2 to left, ready for next oblong cross stitch. Continue in this way to end of row. Work next and subsequent rows below, fitting the oblong cross stitch directly under the cross stitch of the previous row.*

Two=sided Italian cross stitch

Materials Tapestry wool, persian or chunky yarn for a hard-wearing close-textured fabric.
Uses Inset panel for matching rug and cushion set, or all-over pattern for sofa upholstery, chair seat, box-sided pouffe or satchel.

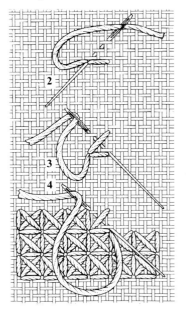

Work from bottom to top in horizontal rows.
1 *Bring yarn through at arrow, insert needle 3 threads to right and bring out at arrow.*
2 *Insert needle diagonally upwards over 3 intersections and bring out again at starting place.*
3 *Insert needle 3 threads up, pass needle diagonally behind 3 intersections and bring out.*
4 *Make diagonal stitch up to left over 3 intersections and bring needle out at starting point, ready to make next stitch. Continue to end of row. Work next row above, where horizontal stitches complete the squares of the previous row*

Plaited gobelin stitch

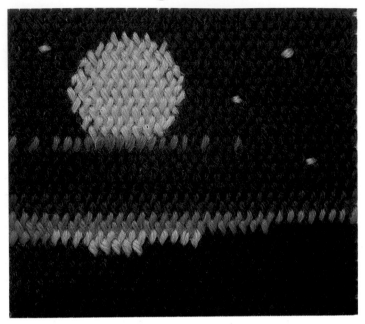

Materials Crewel wool or tapestry yarn for a quick, interwoven filling; plain or random-dyed stranded cotton for a shaded effect.
Uses All-over pattern for landscape cushion set, brick book-end cover or wallet; motif for birthday or wedding anniversary card.

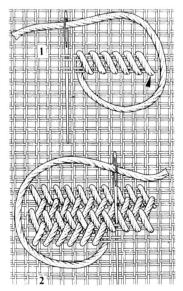

Work horizontally, starting at top right of canvas.
1 Bring yarn out and make a diagonal stitch up over 2 double threads, one double thread to left and bring needle out 2 double threads down. Continue in this way to end of row.
2 On last stitch of first row, bring needle out 3 double threads down. Insert needle diagonally up over 2 double threads, one double thread to right and bring out 2 double threads down. Continue in this way to end of row, overlapping the stitches of the previous row.

Spanish stitch

Materials Stranded cotton, crewel wool or tapestry yarn for a firm, interlocked fabric.

Uses Child's coat yoke or dress inset panel, or all over repeat for shoulder bag or rug; ground stitch for games-table top or soft toy.

1 *Work from left to right. Bring yarn out at top left and make a diagonal stitch up to right over 2 double thread intersections; bring needle out 2 double threads down.*
2 *Make a second diagonal stitch up to left over 2 double threads, one double thread to left, and bring out 2 double threads down. Continue to end of row. Work next and subsequent rows directly below, fitting the top of the stitch into the bottom of the stitch of previous row.*

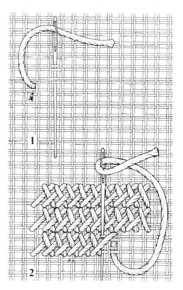

Greek stitch

Materials Persian yarn, carpet thrums or rug wool for quick infilling and criss-cross effect.

Uses Rug and matching cushion inset panel, or all-over stitch for wastepaper-bin cover, work bag, coffee-pot or egg-cosy.

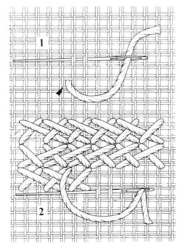

1 *Work from left to right. Bring yarn out and make a diagonal stitch up to right over 2 double thread intersections. Bring needle out 2 double threads to left.*
2 *Make a diagonal stitch down to right over 4 vertical and 2 horizontal double threads. Bring needle out 2 double threads to left. Continue to end of row. Turn canvas upside-down to work second and every alternate row.*

Web stitch

Materials Tapestry wool, persian yarn or carpet thrums for a hard-wearing, seedy-textured fabric.

Uses All-over stitch for simple geometric-patterned photo album cover, backgammon board, church kneeler; fireside rug inset panel or border.

1 *Work diagonally from top left to bottom right. Bring yarn out and make a diagonal stitch up to right over 1 double thread intersection. Bring needle out 1 double thread below starting point. Make a stitch up over 2 double thread intersections, pass needle behind and bring out in between double mesh of first intersection.*
2 *Make a short stitch over the diagonal stitch, inserting the needle in between the double mesh 1 double thread intersection down to right and bring out 1 double thread intersection down to left.*
3 *Continue to increase length of diagonal stitches, arranging crossed stitches so that they alternate evenly with those in previous row.*

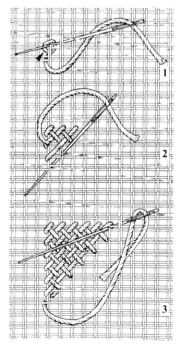

Knotted stitch

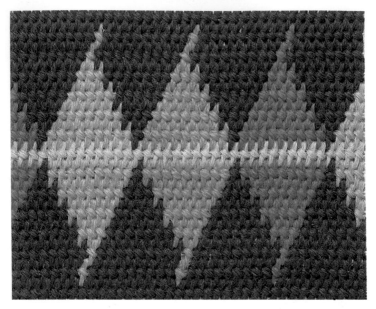

Materials Soft embroidery thread, crewel yarn or tapestry wool for quick and effective infilling.

Uses Background stitch for a simple landscape, still-life or portrait picture, or all-over stitch pattern for belt, curtain ties or cushion set.

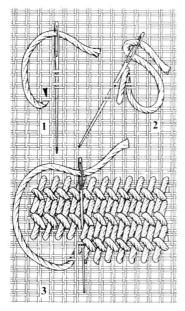

1 *Work horizontally, starting at top right. Bring yarn out and make a diagonal stitch up over 3 double threads and 1 double thread to right. Bring needle out 2 double threads down.*

2 *Insert needle diagonally up over 1 double thread and bring out 2 double threads down and 1 double thread to left.*

3 *Continue to end of row, and repeat below, fitting the long diagonal stitch into the space left in the previous row.*

Herringbone stitch

Materials Tapestry wool or chunky yarn for a very quick filling with a three-dimensional effect.

Uses Background or border repeat for large-scale wall panel; all-over stitch pattern for Christmas stocking, cushion set or bolster.

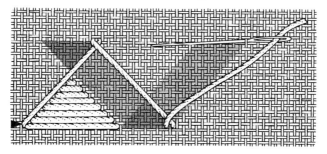

Work horizontally from left to right. Bring yarn out and insert needle 14 threads up and 12 threads to right. Bring needle out 1 thread to left. Insert needle again 14 threads down and 12 threads to right. Continue to end of row. On next row, bring the same, or contrast-coloured, yarn out 1 thread to left of starting point; repeat as for first row. Repeat 8 times more. Work in lower half of diamond in the same way but begin by inserting needle 14 threads down and 12 threads to right. Work inner diamond shape in straight stitches over 1, 3, 5, 7, 9, 11, and 13 threads and in reverse sequence from 11 threads to 1.

Double straight cross stitch

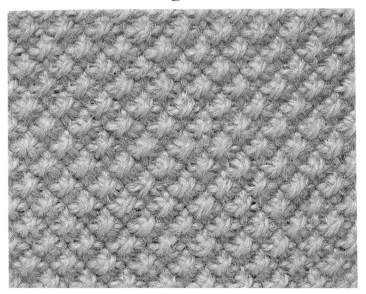

Materials Persian yarn, carpet thrums or chunky knitting wool for a raised bobble effect.

Uses Mix with smooth and embossed stitches for an Aran-look rug and cushion set; all-over repeat for bedroom chair seat or slippers.

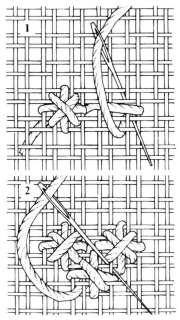

Work the canvas horizontally from left to right.

1 Bring yarn out to left, insert needle 4 threads to right and bring out 2 threads down and 2 to left. Insert needle 4 threads up, bring out 3 threads down and 1 to right.

2 Insert needle diagonally over 2 intersections to left, bring out 2 threads down, re-insert over 2 intersections to right and bring out 1 thread down and 1 to right, ready to work next stitch. Continue in this way to end of row. Work second and every alternate row below, fitting the stitches closely into the triangular shapes made by crosses in the previous row.

STAR STITCHES

Radiating star stitches are easy to work and cover the canvas fast, showing rich textural qualities – from the decorative effect of eyelets, which combine well with other square stitches, the pictorial look of leaf stitch and the illusion of movement in fan stitch, to the beautiful bumpiness of Rhodes stitch.

Star stitch

Materials Tapestry wool, rug thrums or persian yarn for a simple, beginner's piece.

Uses All-over stitch for pincushion, needlebook, curtain ties, guitar strap or napkin ring; satchel or cushion inset panel.

Work horizontally or vertically. Begin at arrow and work a series of straight stitches over 4 horizontal and 4 vertical threads, so as to form an eight-pointed star. Work from the outer edge; insert needle over 2 intersections of thread and make 8 straight stitches, each radiating from the same central hole as shown. Continue to end of row and repeat.

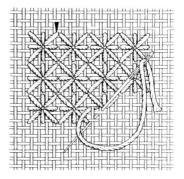

Eye stitch

Materials Chunky rug yarn for a fast filling; soft embroidery thread or fine tapestry wool for a pretty, radiating effect.

Uses Matching bedside rug and bolster panel or work-bag; all-over stitch for chair seat, foot stool or teenager's brick book-end cover.

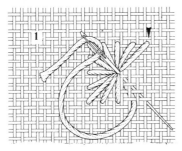

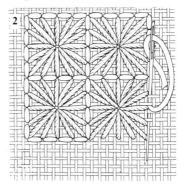

1 *Work either vertically or horizontally. Start at top right corner of star and work a series of 16 straight stitches, all radiating from the same central point, and covering 8 vertical and 8 horizontal threads. Leave 2 threads between each straight stitch.*

2 *Complete required number of eye stitches, and, with a contrast yarn, outline them with a row of back stitches worked over 2 threads.*

Rhodes stitch

Materials Carpet thrums or thick rug wool for a really chunky texture; crewel wool or tapestry yarn for a slightly formal look.
Uses Inset panel or border for Aran-look cushion set, rug or coffee-pot cosy; ground stitch for lamp-base cover, bag, belt or braces.

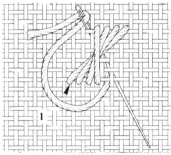

1 *Work vertically or horizontally. Start at bottom left and make a series of diagonal stitches to cover a square of 6 vertical and 6 horizontal threads. Bring yarn out at arrow, insert needle over 6 intersections of thread (AB) and bring out 1 thread to right of arrow. Insert needle again 1 thread to left of previous stitch and bring out 1 thread to right. Continue in this way until the square is filled.*

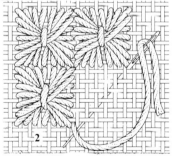

2 *Finish off each square with a small vertical "tying" stitch made over the 2 central threads. Bring yarn out to bottom right corner ready for the next stitch.*

Fan stitch

Materials Medium-weight embroidery thread or tapestry yarn for a fascinating leafy effect.

Uses Motif for picture, wallet or cushion inset panel; repeat pattern for wall-hanging; all-over stitch for envelope purse.

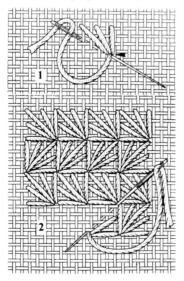

1 Work horizontally or vertically. Start at top left and work a series of 5 radiating straight stitches to form rows of "fan" shapes, each row pointing in an alternate direction. Bring yarn out at arrow, insert needle 4 threads up and bring out again at arrow. Continue in this way to complete the 5 stitches, leaving 2 threads in between each stitch. Bring yarn out 4 threads to right ready to work the next stitch. Continue to the end of the row.

2 Work next and every alternate row in reverse sequence, starting with the bottom threads of the fan.

Leaf stitch

Materials Soft embroidery thread, crewel wool or tapestry yarn for the perfect leaf pattern.

Uses Motif for greetings card, satchel badge or your own house and garden picture; all-over pattern for diary cover.

Work horizontally from left to right. Bring needle out at left, make a diagonal stitch 4 threads down and 3 threads to right and bring out 5 threads up and 3 threads to left. Work 2 more diagonal stitches vertically and bring needle out 5 threads up and 1 thread to right. Insert needle 4 threads down and 2 to right and bring out 5 threads up and 1 thread to right. Insert needle 4 threads down and 1 thread to right, and bring out 5 threads up and 1 thread to right. Insert needle 3 threads down and bring out 2 threads up and 1 thread to right. Work second half of leaf in reverse sequence, and repeat.

St. John's star stitch

Materials Medium to heavy-weight tapestry yarn for a quick, yet intricate-looking, starry pattern.
Uses All-over repeat for bathroom or bedroom rug and matching cushion, slippers, work-bag, egg-cosy set or Christmas stocking.

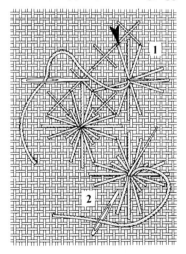

1 *Work horizontally from left to right. Start at top left and work a series of radiating straight stitches, in groups of 3, to form a 4-pointed star, covering 14 threads in both directions. A smaller star is worked into the spaces between and from the same central point. Bring yarn out and work a stitch over 6 threads down and 2 to right. Bring needle out 7 threads up and 2 to right. Insert needle into central point and bring out 5 threads down and 6 to right, ready to work next star point. Repeat 3 times.*
2 *Work 2 diagonal stitches into the 4 spaces left, beginning 3 threads down from the starting point. Complete required number of stars, leaving 2 threads between each one. Work diagonal cross stitches in remaining spaces.*

LOOPED STITCHES

Velvet stitch, or Turkey stitch, is one of the oldest carpet stitches known. Like knot stitch, it is worked first as a loop and then cut and trimmed into a pile finish. The pile may be long or short, depending on the size loop you make, or left simply as an un-cut loop. With longer lengths of yarn, single knot may be used to make a rug fringe. These stitches offer some of the most interesting textures, from loops, cut-pile and fringing to the "knitted" look of chain stitch.

Chain stitch

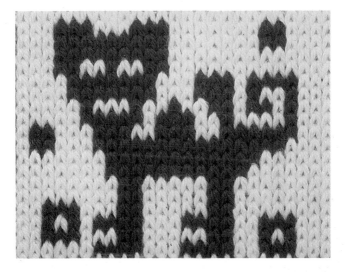

Materials Soft embroidery thread, tapestry wool or persian yarn for a close-textured, hand knitted effect.

Uses Border repeat for child's matching rug and cushion set, or personal egg-cosy, pencil-case or purse motif; all-over stitch for bell pull.

Start at top left and work in vertical rows. Bring yarn out and hold under left thumb. Insert needle into same hole and bring out 2 threads down, draw through loop. Continue in this way to end of row, finishing with a small straight stitch over the last loop.

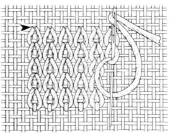

Velvet stitch

Materials Tapestry wool, persian yarn or chunky rug wool for a deep, thick pile.

Uses Child's slippers or dressing-gown pocket motif; all-over stitch for soft toy, pillow or rug.

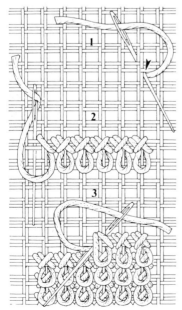

1 *Work horizontally beginning at bottom left. Bring yarn out at arrow, insert needle up to right over 1 double thread intersection and bring out again at arrow.*

2 *Re-insert needle into same hole as before, leaving a loop of yarn at the bottom, or work yarn over a mesh stick. Bring needle out 1 double thread down.*

3 *Take needle up to left over 1 double thread intersection and bring out in same place, ready to make the next stitch. Continue to work required area of loops which may then be cut and trimmed evenly.*

Single knot stitch

Materials Medium to heavy-weight tapestry yarn for a smooth pile; soft embroidery thread for a decorative finish.

Uses Landscape picture motif, or mix with flat stitches for rug and cushion-set embossed pattern; single row for rug or cushion fringe.

1 *Work from left to right, and from the bottom row upwards. Insert needle at arrow and bring out 1 thread up and 2 threads to left. Hold down short end of yarn with left thumb. Insert needle 3 threads to right and bring out 2 threads to left and 1 thread down. Pull yarn tightly downwards to close knot.*

2 *Continue in this way, taking the yarn around a mesh stick, or a knitting needle, to regulate the size of the loops. Work subsequent rows 1 thread up.*

3 *Complete the knotting and then cut and trim the loops evenly.*

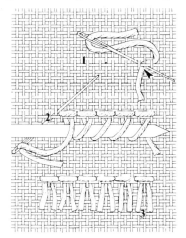

Eastern stitch

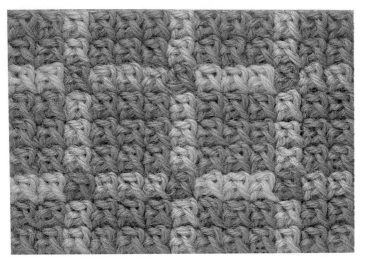

Materials Soft embroidery thread, crewel wool or tapestry yarn for quick, decorative infilling.

Uses Cushion inset panel, or all-over stitch pattern for work-bag, door-stop, coffee-pot cosy, or large-scale motif for wall decoration.

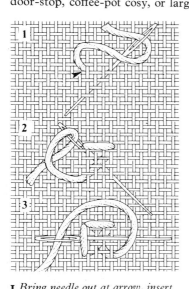

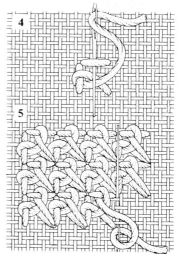

1 *Bring needle out at arrow, insert 4 threads to right, bring out 4 intersections down to left.*
2 *Re-insert needle at arrow; bring out 4 intersections down to right.*
3 *Pass needle under vertical stitch to form a loop, as shown.*

4 *Pass needle under horizontal stitch to form a second loop.*
5 *Insert needle at bottom right of stitch, bring out 4 threads up ready for next stitch. Work subsequent rows directly below, fitting stitches into spaces of previous row.*

Shell stitch

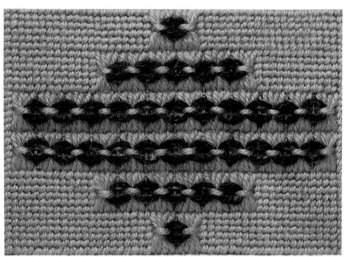

Materials Soft embroidery or stranded cotton, crewel wool or tapestry yarn for a pretty, raised band effect.

Uses Dress yoke or inset panel; border repeat for tassel-tied belt, napkin ring, picture frame or cushion, or large motif infilling.

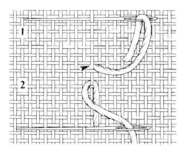

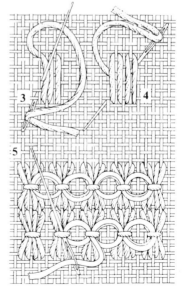

1 *Work horizontally, starting at top right. Bring yarn out at arrow, insert needle 6 threads up and bring out 1 thread to left.*
2 *Insert needle 6 threads down, bring out 1 thread to left.*
3 *Repeat, bring needle out 3 threads up and 1 to right.*
4 *Insert needle 1 thread to right, bring out 3 intersections down to left, ready for next stitch.*
5 *With contrast thread, begin at right. Pass needle down through first back stitch, up through second, down through first again, up through second and on, to complete the row.*

Rococo stitch

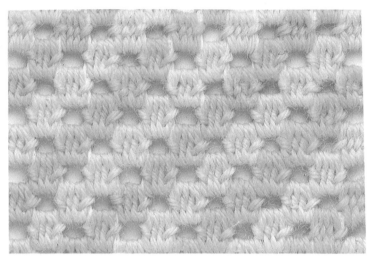

Materials Tapestry wool, persian yarn or rug thrums for a firm, yet delicate-looking filling.

Uses Bedside rug or cushion inset panel; all-over pattern for herb pillow or purse, or mix with Rhodes and velvet stitch for a sporty-look cushion set.

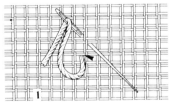

1 *Work diagonally, starting at bottom right. Bring yarn out at arrow, insert needle 2 double threads up and bring out 1 double thread intersection down to right.*
2 *Insert needle 1 double thread to left and bring out 1 down.*
3 *With yarn to left, insert needle 2 double threads up, bring out 1 down.*
4 *Repeat step 2 and make 2 more stitches into the same space.*
5 *Insert needle over 1 double thread to left and bring out 2 double threads down, ready to make the next stitch. Continue to end of row.*
6 *Work subsequent rows diagonally from the top fitting each stitch neatly into the spaces left in the previous row.*

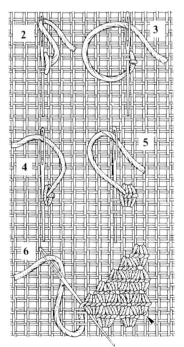

COLOUR STITCH PATTERNS

Colour stitch patterns may be
embroidered either by counting the stitches as you
work the colours in repeat, or by charting them
on graph paper first (see p.10). Patterns repeating in
more than 2 colours are usually established at the beginning.
Work a few stitches in each colour leaving the yarn
pulled through into the canvas margin, ready to
pick up as required.

Chequer stitch

Materials Crewel wool or tapestry yarn for a bright, firmly-woven fabric; soft embroidery or stranded cotton for a beginner's piece.
Uses Scatter cushion inset panel, or all-over pattern for mirror-frame, or cigarette-lighter cover; lavender sachet or pencil-case.

Work horizontally from left to right. Work a series of alternating squares of diagonal stitch and tent stitch. Each square covers 4 horizontal and 4 vertical threads. Begin at top left, and, working every other square, make 7 diagonal stitches in sequence over 1, 2, 3, 4, 3, 2 and 1 intersections of thread. Fill remaining squares with 16 tent stitches; all chequer stitches arranged in colour sequence.

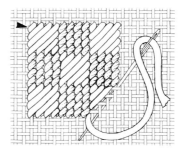

Jacquard stitch

Materials Embroidery thread, crewel wool or tapestry yarn for a formal, brocade effect.

Uses Background stitch for large wall decoration; cushion or rug inset panel, or all-over repeat for bolster, piano stool cover, upholstered ottonman, stool top or box-sided pouffe.

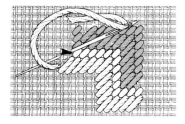

Work diagonally from top left to bottom right and vice versa. Begin at arrow with first colour, and work 5 diagonal stitches to right over 1 double thread intersection; followed by 5 diagonal stitches worked vertically downwards. Continue to end of row. With second colour, begin at bottom right and work 5 diagonal stitches to left over 2 double thread intersections, as shown; followed by 5 diagonal stitches worked vertically upwards. Continue to end of row and repeat.

Moorish stitch

Materials Fine to medium-weight tapestry yarn for a multi-coloured stripy effect.

Uses Rug or floor-cushion inset panel, or mixed-stitch "sampler"; all-over pattern for matching shoulder bag and envelope purse, diary or magazine cover.

Work diagonally starting at top right. Bring yarn out at arrow and work 4 diagonal stitches in sequence over 1, 2, 3, and 2 double thread intersections, and continue in this way to end of row. Work further rows in colour sequence, leaving 1 double thread between each row. With contrast yarn, complete the zigzag line between the rows with small diagonal stitches worked over 1 double thread intersection.

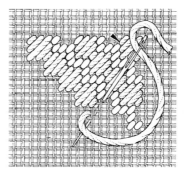

Scottish stitch

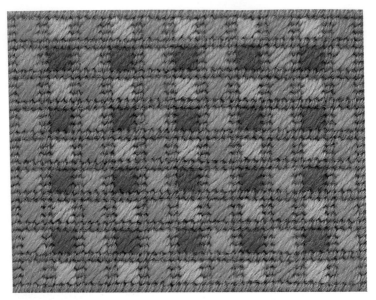

Materials Medium to heavy-weight tapestry yarn for a firmly woven, tartan effect; silk or stranded cotton for a pretty, plaid look.
Uses Cushion set border or inset panel, or all-over repeat for chair seat and back upholstery, satchel or serviette ring; dress yoke, or inset panel, belt, small pincushion, needlebook or watch-strap.

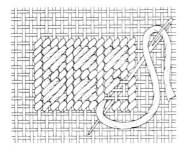

Work horizontally in rows from left to right. Begin by working 5 diagonal stitches in sequence over 1, 2, 3, 2, and 1 intersections of thread, to form a square. Work in the colours shown and repeat, leaving 1 thread between each square and between each row worked. Complete the pattern by outlining the squares in tent stitch.

Leaf pattern

Materials Tapestry wool, persian yarn or chunky rug wool for a shadowy, checkered effect; embroidery thread for a pretty filling.
Uses Chair seat or rug inset panel, or all-over pattern for stool top, shoulder bag, bolster or tea-cosy; powder compact cover, purse, or sunglasses case.

1 *Work diagonally from top left to bottom right. Bring needle out at arrow and work a series of 24 straight stitches made at right angles to each other, with a back stitch worked over each group of 6 stitches. Each "leaf" covers 12 threads in both directions. Work 3 horizontal straight stitches over 1, 2 and 3 threads. Bring needle out 3 threads up and work 3 vertical stitches over 3, 2 and 1 threads.*
2 *Bring needle out at top left and make a back stitch down over 3 intersections of thread. Work 3 more colours in this way, increasing the length of the straight stitches until 12 threads are covered, and the square complete. Continue to end of row. Work next and every alternate row in contrast colours.*

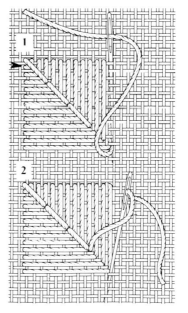

Mosaic stitch pattern

Materials Medium-weight tapestry wool, persian yarn or carpet thrums for a firmly woven fabric.

Uses Inset panel for stool top, sofa upholstery, church kneeler or pouffe; all-over pattern for picture frame, spectacle case or wallet.

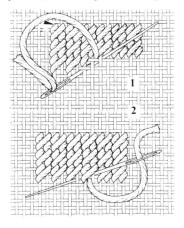

1 *Work horizontally from left to right. Starting at top left make a diagonal stitch down to left over 1 intersection of thread, bring needle out 2 threads to right and 1 thread up. Insert needle down over 2 intersections and bring out 3 threads to right and 2 threads up. Continue to end of row.*

2 *Work second row from right to left, fitting small diagonal stitches into the spaces left on the previous row. Continue to work rows of 5 mosaic stitches in colour sequence. Complete the pattern by working vertical rows of 5 stitches in colour sequence, as shown.*

Oblong cross with backstitch pattern

Materials Crewel wool, tapestry or persian yarn for a simple zigzag effect; soft embroidery thread for mounting under glass.
Uses Workbox lid or cushion inset panel; all-over repeat for Christmas stocking or box-sided window seat cushion.

1 *Begin by working downwards from top left to bottom right. Bring yarn out, insert needle 3 double threads down and 1 double thread to left, and bring out 3 double threads up.*
2 *Insert needle 3 double threads down and 1 to right and bring out 1 double thread to left.*
3 *Re-insert needle over double thread to right and bring out 3 double threads up and 1 to right, and repeat.*
4 *Bring needle out 1 double thread to right ready to make next stitch below. Continue in this way, stepping pairs of stitches in zigzag sequence; work in reverse direction every 7 blocks, and in colours shown.*

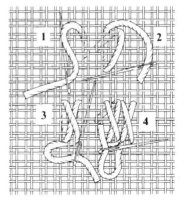

Florentine stitch

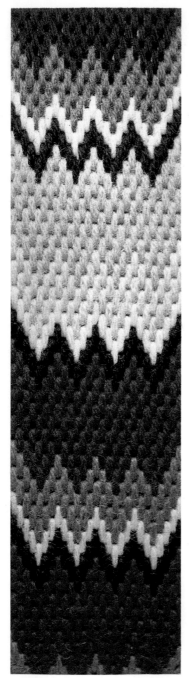

Materials Soft embroidery thread, tapestry wool or persian yarn for the bargello pattern.

Uses Cushion set border, or inset panel for stitch sample "patchwork" rug or bolster; all-over repeat for belt or braces.

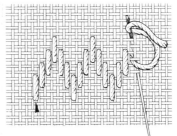

Work horizontally, bringing yarn out at left. Insert needle 4 threads up and bring out 2 threads down and 1 to right. Continue in this way to work 3 more stitches, each one 4 threads up and 2 back; then work 3 stitches, 4 threads down and 2 up, to end of row.

BARGELLO PATTERNS

*Typified by subtle tonal gradations, Bargello gets
its name from the Bargello Palace in Florence, where
beautiful pieces of this embroidery are displayed. These
patterns are generally easy to work after establishing the
foundation row. Patterns include zigzags and curves,
pinnacles, pomegranate and honeycomb.*

Pinnacled curves

Materials Crewel wool, tapestry or persian yarn for the traditional
"tapestry" finish.
Uses All-over design for matching window pelmet and curtain ties,
dining chair seat, stool top; satchel or envelope purse inset panel.

*Work varying steps of vertical
stitches over 6 threads and back
under 3; repeat in reverse every 21
stitches by 7 rows of colour.*

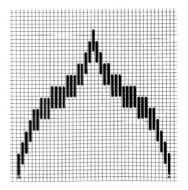

Zigzags and pinnacles

Materials Medium-weight embroidery thread, crewel or tapestry wool oddments for simple practice points.

Uses Repeat pattern for sunglasses or pencil-case, stitch sampler, belt or braces.

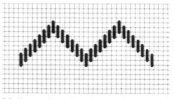

Make a simple zigzag *in stepped vertical stitches over 3 threads and back under 2; repeat every 14 stitches across by 3 rows of colour.*

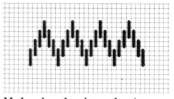

Make simple pinnacles *by working stepped vertical stitches over 4 threads and back under 2; repeat every 6 stitches across by 4 rows of colour.*

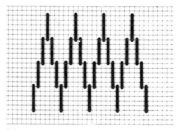

Make taller pinnacles *by working stepped vertical stitches over 6 threads and back under 1; repeat every 6 stitches across by 5 rows of colour.*

Stepped zigzags and steep pinnacles

Materials Medium-weight yarns or knitting wools for developing your stitch technique.
Uses All-over design for comb or spectacles case, wall-hanging stitch sampler or folding luggage-rack straps.

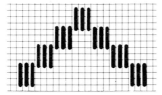

Make simple, stepped zigzags *in blocks of 3 vertical stitches made over 4 threads and back under 1; repeat every 18 stitches across by 4 rows of colour.*

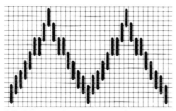

Make gently curved zigzags *by working stepped vertical stitches, and blocks of 2 stitches, over 5 threads and back under 2, 5 threads and back under 3, and over 5 threads and back under 4; repeat every 16 stitches across by 5 rows of colour.*

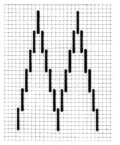

Make very tall pinnacles *by working stepped vertical stitches over 6 threads and back under 1; repeat every 10 stitches across by 8 rows of colour.*

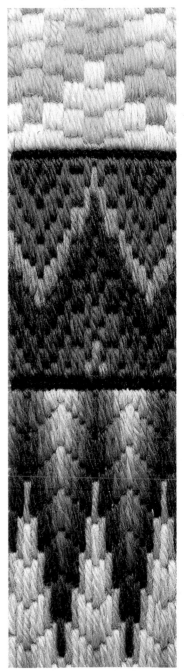

Diagonal pinnacles

Materials Medium-weight tapestry or persian yarn for a softly-shaded, stripe effect.

Uses Background pattern for large-scale wall decoration, cushion or workbag inset panel; all-over pattern for chair seat.

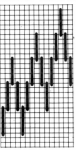

Work stepped vertical stitches over 6 threads and back under 1; repeat every 5 stitches across by 5 rows of colour.

Stepped diagonal pinnacles

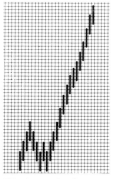

Work varying steps of vertical stitches over 6 threads and back under 3, to form diagonal rows; repeat every 23 stitches across by 7 rows of colour.

Materials Tapestry yarn with silk or lurex highlights for dramatic-looking, broken stripe effect.

Uses Floor pillow or scatter cushion inset panel, or all-over pattern for lamp-base cover, desk diary or photo album cover.

Gothic pinnacles

Materials Medium-weight tapestry or persian yarn for a bold masculine pattern.

Uses Inset panel for fireside rug and matching cushion set, or all-over pattern for shaped bed-head panel, chair or sofa upholstery.

Work regularly stepped stitches over 6, and 2 threads, back under 1, respectively; repeat in 8 colours.

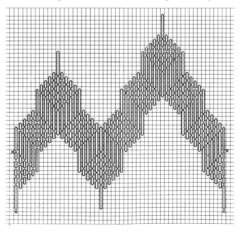

Curves

Materials Soft embroidery thread, crewel wool or tapestry yarn for a simple stripy pattern.
Uses Leather-trimmed carpet-bag panel, or all-over design for a flat cushion pad, tennis racket cover or circular pouffe.

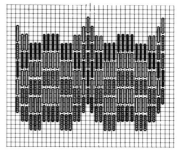

Work stepped vertical stitches over 4 threads and back under 2; repeat every 17 stitches across and in 13 colours as shown.

Undulating pinnacles

Materials Medium-weight tapestry yarn for a zigzaggy effect.
Uses Satchel or rug inset panel; all-over pattern for waistcoat front, wide belt, wallet or box-sided window-seat pads.

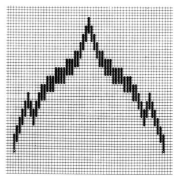

Work varying steps of vertical stitches over 6 threads and back under 3; repeat every 53 stitches across by 8 rows of colour.

Pomegranate

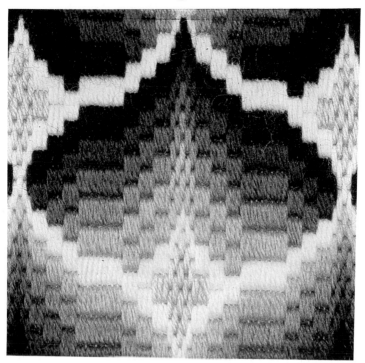

Materials Tapestry wool, persian yarn or rug thrums for a bold figurative finish.

Uses Rug or floor-cushion inset panel; all-over design for bolster or director's folding-chair seat and back panel.

Work varying steps of vertical stitches over 6 threads and back under 3. Stitch basic "curved" foundation row across canvas and then stitch a second row in reverse. Fill in the resulting pomegranate shapes, repeated in 7 colours.

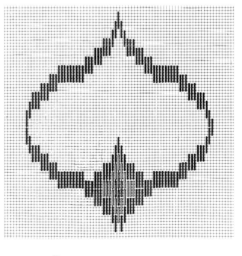

Pinnacles with wells

Materials Soft embroidery thread or medium-weight tapestry yarn for a firm, zingy-patterned fabric; stranded cotton or silk for added dazzle.

Uses All-over repeat for wall picture, chair seat, or sofa bolster; dress yoke or inset panel, bolero, pocket or purse pattern.

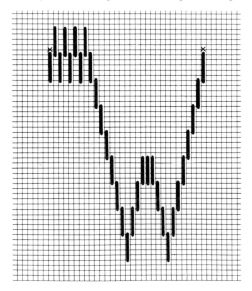

Work stepped vertical stitches over 6 threads and back under 1; repeat every 30 stitches across by 7 rows of colour.

Pinnacles with stripes

Materials Crewel wool, tapestry yarn, persian wool or rug thrums for a strongly banded pattern.

Uses All-over repeat for long window-seat cushion, bed-head panel, or french window pelmet and matching curtain ties.

Work pinnacles in stepped vertical stitches over 6 threads and back under 2; repeat every 56 stitches across by 7 rows of colour. Work stripes in vertical straight stitches over 2, 3, and 4 threads; repeat in 3 colours.

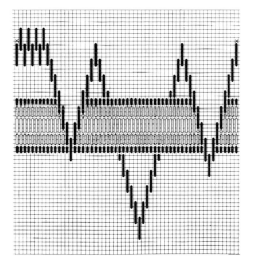

Chevron trellis

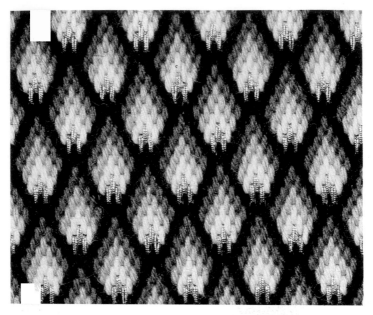

Materials Fine crewel wool or tapestry yarn with lurex for a richly-textured fabric.

Uses Inset panel for plain, box-sided cushion set; all-over design for bolero, evening bag, guitar strap, belt or braces.

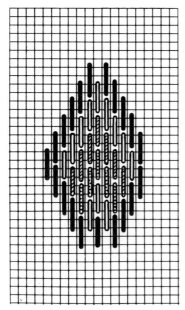

Work stepped vertical stitches over 4 threads and back under 2; repeat every 28 stitches across and in 5 colours.

Mirror image pinnacles

Materials Crewel wool, tapestry or persian yarn for a firm, hard-wearing fabric.

Uses Inset panel for matching rug and cushion set; all-over repeat for long foot stool, chair upholstery, door-stop or wallet.

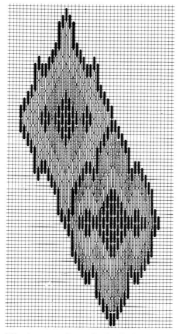

Work stepped vertical stitches over 3, 4, 6 and 8 threads, using 7 colours.

Mirror image chevron and pinnacles

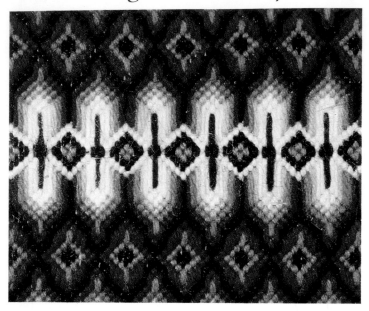

Materials Medium-weight tapestry wool, persian yarn or rug thrums for a strongly-banded effect.

Uses Background pattern for large wall decoration, or all-over design for bolster, herb pillow, slippers or clutch bag.

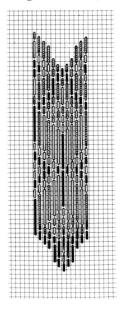

Work stepped vertical stitches in pattern, over 6 threads back under 1, 3 threads back under 1, and 2 threads back under 1; repeat every 12 stitches across, and downwards in reverse pattern sequence, in 6 colours as shown.

Honeycomb

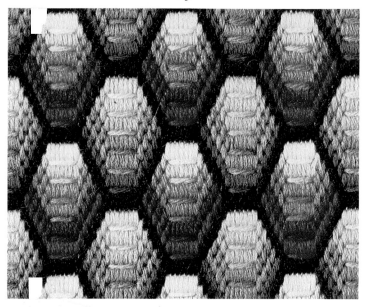

Materials Crewel wool, tapestry yarn or rug thrums for a firm, boldly patterned fabric.

Uses Floor-cushion or rug inset panel; all-over pattern for hexagonal box-sided cushion set, dining chair seat, work-bag or satchel.

Work stepped vertical stitches over 4 threads and back under 2, for main honeycomb pattern. Work blocks of vertical stitches over 4 threads, with horizontal straight stitches between, to complete each honeycomb; repeat pattern in 13 colours.

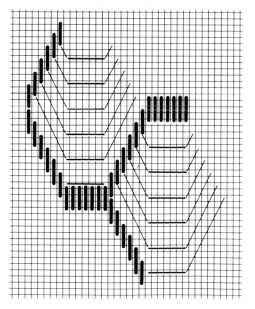

Four=way Florentine pattern

Materials Medium-weight tapestry yarn for a closely-woven, classic-style fabric.

Uses Inset panel for scatter cushion set or bed-head hanging pillows; repeat motif for window-seat pads, bedside rug or shoulder bag.

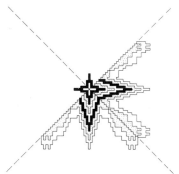

In working towards the centre, *first mark canvas with diagonal lines in both directions. Work foundation row, on outer edge of all 4 sections, in varying steps of vertical stitches, over 4 threads and back under 2; work inwards and repeat in colour sequence as shown.*

In working outwards from the centre, *first mark canvas with diagonal lines in both directions. Begin at the centre with 4 straight stitches, placed at right angles to each other. Work vertical stitches over 4 threads and back under 2, and develop each quarter of pattern evenly, as you work outwards in colour sequence as shown.*

BORDERS

*Simple decorative borders can be added to needlepoint,
either by counting the stitches in pattern as you go, or
by working from a chart. The side sections of a desk blotter
may be worked separately before attaching them to the
blotter pad, whereas a "picture-frame" border
is best worked on a rectangular piece of
canvas, cutting away the inside area
before making up.*

Interlacing

Materials Soft embroidery thread, crewel wool or tapestry yarn for
a classic-style finish.

Uses Border for games-table, matching bedside rug and bolster,
bell pull, desk blotter, mirror frame, or belt.

Cross stitch

Stripes

Materials Medium-weight tapestry yarn for a quickly worked edging.

Uses Border for picture frame or cushion set, belt or hat-band; repeat in vertical stripes for wastebin cover.

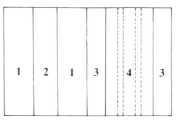

1 **Straight stitch**
2 **Raised chain band**
3 **Double cross stitch**
4 **Straight stitch with back stitch**

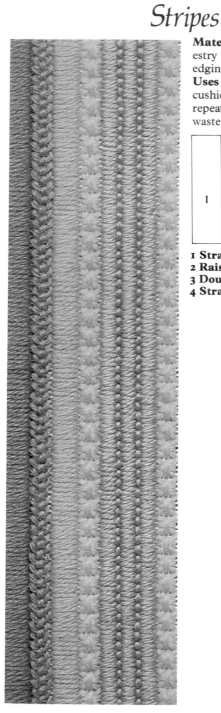

"Aran"

Materials Tapestry wool, rug thrums or chunky yarn for a deep, embossed effect.

Uses Border for Aran-type or plain-coloured cushion set or rug, shoulder bag, coffee-pot cosy or bolster.

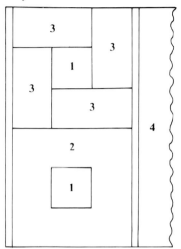

1 Rhodes stitch
2 Chequer stitch
3 Upright Gobelin stitch
4 Single knot stitch

Diamonds

Materials Soft embroidery thread, crewel wool or tapestry yarn for a bold, geometric finish.
Uses Border for desk blotter, mirror frame, stool top, or floor cushion; folding luggage-rack straps, thong-tied belt or serviette ring.

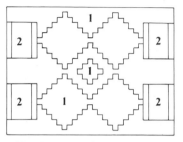

1 Vertical straight stitch
2 Horizontal straight stitch

Leaf

Materials Tapestry wool for a pretty, delicate edging; fine embroidery thread or silk for a keepsake quality.

Uses Border for picture frame or bed-head panel, pattern for belt, bell pull, braces or napkin ring; christening or wedding anniversary card, bookmark or watch-strap.

Tent stitch

MITRED CORNERS

*Corners can be mitred by drawing a diagonal line
across the corner of your chart and by repeating the
border image on the opposite side.*

Harlequin corner

Materials Soft embroidery thread or fine
tapestry wool for a pretty, geometric finish.
Uses Border for keepsake picture, herb
pillow, photo frame, scatter cushion, valentine or greetings card.

Persian rug corner

Materials Crewel wool or tapestry yarn for a traditional-style
rug border.
Uses Matching rug and cushion
set, sofa pillow or stool top;
satchel inset panel, picture frame
or carpetbag border.

Index

Acknowledgments

Contributors
Gisela Banbury
Jackie Binns
J and P Coats (Glasgow)
Janet Haigh
Eileen Lowcock
Lesley Prescott
The Royal School
of Needlework (London)
Louise Stern
Janet Swift

Photographers
Ian O'Leary
Steve Oliver

Artists
John Hutchinson
David Ashby
Gary Marsh

Typesetting
Contact Graphics Ltd

Reproduction
F E Burman Ltd